WHISPERS OF CHAI, ECHOES OF WHISKEY

A MAN'S JOURNEY THROUGH LOVE, LOSS, AND REDEMPTION

UHAN BARMAN

Made with ♥ on the Notion Press Platform
www.notionpress.com

Whiskey and Chai explores life's complexities through poems. Like the contrasting flavours of the drinks, the collection delves into unexpected love, the fight against injustice, defying societal pressures, the strength of family, and the bittersweet mix of life's experiences. It's a raw and emotional journey celebrating the human spirit.

Contents

Contents

Contents

Foreword

Life, like a perfectly brewed cup of chai, is a blend of complex flavors. The comforting warmth of love and connection mingles with the bitter sting of loss and betrayal. Yet, a dash of the unexpected, a hint of defiance, can create a symphony of emotions that lingers on the tongue long after the last sip.

"Whiskey and Chai" is an invitation to savor this symphony. Here, you'll find poems that explore the raw and unfiltered struggles of the human experience. The verses grapple with the weight of societal expectations, the searing pain of false accusations, and the enduring love between a father and child.

But amidst the darkness, there's light. Unexpected connections blossom, offering solace and a glimmer of hope. The poems celebrate the courage to break free from traditional molds and embrace vulnerability. Each line is a testament to the resilience of the human spirit, a spirit that finds strength in family, fights for justice, and dares to love again.

As you delve into these poems, prepare to be stirred, not shaken. Allow the words to wash over you, to evoke memories, challenge assumptions, and perhaps even ignite a spark of rebellion within your own soul. For within this collection lies not just a story, but a reflection – a reflection of the bittersweet beauty that is life itself.

So, raise a metaphorical glass, whether it be filled with the comforting warmth of chai or the smoky allure of whiskey, and prepare to embark on a journey of self-discovery through the evocative verses of "Whiskey and Chai."

Preface

Life simmers with experiences, as diverse and unexpected as the ingredients in a steaming cup of chai or a well-aged whiskey. This collection of poems offers a taste of that intricate blend, exploring the complexities of love, loss, societal pressures, and the unwavering fight for justice.

There are no sugar-coated tales here. These verses delve into the raw emotions that color our lives – the sting of betrayal, the unexpected melody of love found in unlikely places, the frustration of battling injustice, and the unwavering strength found in family bonds.

Each poem is a brushstroke, painting a vibrant tapestry of the human experience. Some may leave you with a lingering warmth, like the comforting aroma of cardamom, while others might evoke a smoky intensity, mirroring the challenges we face.

Prepare to be stirred, not shaken, as you journey through these verses. Allow the poems to resonate with your own experiences, to challenge your perspectives, and perhaps even offer a newfound appreciation for the bittersweet symphony of life itself.

Let the poems of "Whiskey and Chai" be your companion on this introspective journey.

Acknowledgements

Thanks to family, friends, and anyone who's ever felt lost. This book's for you. Special thanks to the editor and readers for picking up the book.

Prologue

Close your eyes. Imagine the aroma of warm spices swirling in the air, the comforting steam of a freshly brewed chai. Now, picture the sharp bite of a well-aged whiskey, a drink that lingers on the tongue long after the last sip.

"Whiskey and Chai" is not a single flavor, but a complex blend. It's the bittersweet symphony of life, where love and loss intertwine like the heady cardamom in your chai and the smoky allure of your whiskey.

Prepare to embark on a journey through emotions. You'll taste the sting of betrayal, the unexpected sweetness of love found in forgotten corners, and the simmering anger of injustice. But within these pages, you'll also find the unwavering strength of family bonds, the courage to defy expectations, and the enduring spirit that fights for what's right.

So, take a deep breath, let the emotions wash over you, and allow these poems to stir your soul. For within this collection lies not just a story, but a reflection – a reflection of the bittersweet beauty that is life itself.

1. The Birth

In a world of shadows, a man is born, From the womb of night, into the morn. His cries echo through the silent air, As he enters a realm of joy and despair.
Tiny fingers grasp at the unknown, His journey of life, newly sown. But the path ahead, rugged and steep, Where dreams may wither, and hopes may weep.
With each breath drawn, he learns to fight, Against the darkness, to seek the light. For he's now tasked with a

daunting role, To navigate through life's turbulent shoal.
Though storms may rage and winds may blow, His spirit is
resilient, he'll come to know. For in his heart, a flame burns
bright, Guiding him through the darkest night.
With each step forward, he'll find his way, Facing the world
with courage each day. For in the birth of a man, a tale is
spun, Of resilience, strength, and battles won.

2. From womb to staring back at her eyes

In hushed tones, a world unknown, A symphony of touch and moan. A face, a blur, a voice so near, A lullaby to banish fear.

Then, light unfurls, a tapestry bright, A face emerges, bathed in light. Eyes like pools, a gentle smile, My mother's love, a sacred isle.

Each curve, each line, a story told, Wrinkles etched, where laughter bold, Has chased away the passing years, A map of love that conquers fears.

I reach, a hand, so small and new, To touch this face, forever true. Warmth meets warmth, a silent vow, This world unveiled, I see her now.

No longer just a voice, a touch, But here she is, I love her so much. A teardrop falls, a glistening bead, The first sight seen, a love decreed.

3. The distance from him

"As we grew older, we saw the monster in each other, bridges burnt from hands, a voice mute from within"

Tiny hands, a baseball glove, Sunlight dappled, chasing love. Walks by streams, a whispered joke, Bond of branches, firmly yoked.

Teenage whispers, headphones tight, Worlds unseen, bathed in screen light. Dinner silence stretched thin, Words unspoken, locked within.

Shadows lengthen, voices low, and Questions rise, but never flow. Giant strides, a slamming door, Distance grows, what was before?

A faded glove, a dusty frame, Memories whisper of a name. A silent yearning, bittersweet, For fields of laughter, at his feet.

Grayscale silence, years unwind, Aching space where hearts entwined. Hope remains, a whispered plea, To bridge the gap, and finally see.

4. A war within

• 5 •

"Uncertainty is a war, battles are meant to lose"

A war within, a changing tide, Body revolts, can't keep it inside. Mirrored reflection, a stranger's stare, Longing to fit, but never quite there.
Friendships are a puzzle, pieces don't fit, and Fear of rejection is a constant pit. Laughter and secrets, whispered and shared, But is it real, or just a facade compared?
Grades become battles, victories sought, Pressure to win, a heavy thought. Doubt whispers questions, a relentless hum, "Am I enough?" the answer numb.
Dreams take flight, on wings unsure, The future's a canvas, the path obscure. Choices to make, a winding maze, Lost in the moment, searching for ways.
Parents like mountains, unmovable, strong, Their expectations, a relentless song. Craving freedom, a voice to be heard, But the bridge of respect sometimes feels absurd.
A storm in a teacup, emotions run high, and A single harsh word can bring tears to an eye. Vulnerability is hidden, a mask to portray, The weight of the world, in a single day.
But beneath the turmoil, a strength takes hold, A fire within, a story untold. This is the season, to learn and to grow,

Through the chaos and confusion, a future will flow.

5. When I first met Mr. Depression & Miss anxiety

A shadow creeps, unseen, unheard, A weight descends, a whispered word. A heart that fluttered, light and free, Now trapped in a cage, with a heavy key.

The world, once vibrant, loses its hue, Laughter is a ghost, replaced by a blue. Thoughts, like dark clouds, gather and loom, Whispering doubts in the quiet room.

Simple tasks, a mountain's might, Breathing shallow, a suffocating night. Friends' smiling faces, a distant scene, Loneliness whispers, "You're not unseen."

Tears come unbidden, a salty stream, The future a question, a broken dream. What lurks inside, a monster unknown, Gripping so tight, it feels all alone.

This is the storm, the first taste of fear, Anxiety's grip, and depression's tear. But know this, dear heart, though darkness may reign, The sun will rise again, and hope will sustain. You are not broken, though shadows may fall, A strength resides within you, to conquer it all. Reach out a hand, and let kindness ignite, There's help in the light, to heal and take flight.

This is your journey, a path to explore, Embrace the darkness, and find the light's core. For courage is found in facing the fight, And emerging stronger, bathed in morning's light.

6. The heartache

*"In the era of stones, when hearts were made of
helium and paper boats"*

In crowded hallways, a stolen glance, A blush that blooms
with a nervous chance. Across the classroom, a secret smile,
Butterflies flutter, and a heart runs wild.
Pencils tap softly, a whispered rhyme, Passing notes hidden, a
way to unwind. Lunchtime is stolen, beneath the old oak,
Shy conversations, a world we evoke.
Shared dreams whispered, on whispered breeze, Homework
forgotten, beneath the leaves. Stolen glances, a shy hello, A
world of "maybes," a love that can grow.
Stolen chocolate, a sticky delight, Sharing earbuds, listening
all night. Giggles erupt, a playful fight, and Innocence
blooms, in the golden light.
The first name scribbled, on a notebook page, A hidden
message, a love's sweet cage. Passing notes folded, a secret
confessed, A shy "I like you," puts love to the test.
School dances awkward, a nervous sway, A stolen handhold,
takes us away. Fumbling steps, beneath the disco ball, Young
hearts aflutter, risking it all.

The taste of bubblegum, a stolen kiss, A fleeting moment, a world of bliss. Teenage love stories, whispered and true, Innocent dreams, in the morning dew.

7. The heartbreak

"It felt like a needle piercing a beating pound of meat"

A shattered mirror, the world cracks in two, and Yesterday's laughter is replaced by blue. Your name, a whisper, a ghost in the breeze, Empty laughter rings, mocking at ease. Memories dance, a bittersweet sting, Of stolen glances, the joy you would bring. Promises whispered, like dreams in the night, Now scattered like ashes, lost in the light.
A playground of joy now feels cold and bare, Swings creak in silence, a weight in the air. Songs once so happy, bring tears to my eyes, Haunted by echoes of shared butterflies.
Anger flares hot, then melts into ache, A heavy silence, a heart that can't break. But deeper within, a flicker remains, A strength yet to rise, through the pouring rain.
This love, a lesson, though painful and raw, Taught the language of yearning, the sting of the claw. It showed me the beauty, the depths of the soul, And the courage it takes, to let someone go.
The path stretches onward, a future unknown, But the lessons I've learned will help me grow. With a tear-stained smile, I'll rise from the fall, For even the first heartbreak, can

make you stand tall.

8. Where's the bullet

"Bullying is an act of a coward, some see through it some live with it, the consequences are to both who hold the gun and takes the bullet"

Scornful laughter, a pointed barb, Words like missiles, leaving their scar. Lunch in the shadows, a silent retreat, Wishing for invisibility, a place to be neat.
They called me "Oddball," a different kind, My quiet ways, left them far behind. Tempting whispers, a devilish grin, "Join the rebellion, and let the fun begin."
Spray paint cans glisten, mischief in tow, School walls defaced, a destructive flow. A thrill of acceptance, a fleeting embrace, Ignoring the tremor, the guilt in my face.
Caught red-handed, punishment swift, Parents' faces, disappointment adrift. Detention's isolation, a chance to reflect, The cost of belonging, a heavy defect.
Standing alone, tears stain my cheek, Was acceptance worth, the heart I did speak? The kindness I treasured, turned sour and mean, Real friends see you, not the one you can't be.
Lessons etched deep, a scar on my soul, True strength lies in you, to take back control. A voice long suppressed rises with might, "I will not be broken, I'll choose what is right."

The path to redemption, a journey to mend, Building bridges, with those I can defend. A heart bruised but healing, a spirit set free, True worth comes from within, the best version of me.

9. And you met him

"He wore a simple attire, very simpler than most filters I bear. A glass of friendship we share"

A solitary journey, a path walked alone, Yearning for connection, a heart made of stone. Faces blurred by, a whisper, a smile, But never a feeling, to stay for a while. Then a spark ignited, a laugh that took flight, Two souls intertwined, bathed in warm light. Secrets unfurled, like petals so bright, Vulnerability shared, in the welcoming night.

Disagreements rumble, like storms in the sky, But honesty bridges, tears never deny. Laughter rings true, a melody shared, Joys and sorrows whispered, a burden unbarred. Comfort's embrace, in moments of strife, A hand to hold tight, through the battles of life. Distance may stretch, oceans may roar, But the bond remains strong, forevermore.

This, is the essence, of friendship's sweet grace, A mirror reflecting, your truest face. No judgment they cast, no need to pretend, Just acceptance and love, till the very end. So raise a glass high, to these kindred spirits, A treasure more precious, than any merit. For in their presence, the world feels anew, This, my dear friend, is the magic of you.

10. Knowing the unknowking

"And I seek myself in the mirror now, I see an ugly man, I start grooming it once again"

A bud unfurls, a slow ballet, Unseen by eyes, day by day. We dream of change, a grand display, But growth, it whispers, a different way.

We wrench at the stem, impatient and raw, Wanting the flower, to burst without flaw. But nature's wisdom, unseen by law, Nurtures the process, with a silent "haw."

The sun's gentle kiss, a whisper of rain, The patient pull of the earth's soft domain. These unseen forces, ease away pain, As strength builds within, in the sun and rain.

We crave the butterfly, wings bright and grand, But forget the struggle, the shift in the sand. The chrysalis holds, a form misunderstood, Yet within it transforms, a creature renewed.

So let us embrace, the slow, steady climb, The shedding of skin, one precious chime. For growth is a journey, that takes its own time, A beautiful dance, in the rhythm of rhyme.

With patience and care, like the sculptor's embrace, We chip away at flaws and find beauty's true space. The lessons we learn, at a gradual pace, Shape who we become, with enduring grace.

11. So far

So far, it's said it's "you" glory or "failure" an intangible journey silence sacrifices and share. Uncertainty at its peak as we speak you are the man that everyone seeks, including you, "yourself" chiselling bones and muscles along with scars and soul. A young man stepping into the storm gaining knowledge about the wicked hearts born. You saw the world kind and ruthless isn't it any less than a war on the borderline?

Or do you choose to join the line?

A man is an animal born from a kind heart torn to pieces if not predator that's what the world carves, nevertheless the burden is taken and sow not all pain quantified and a bore.

We are just becoming a man.

12. The hollow

"Pain starts here, wear your armour"

Shoulders squared a stoic mask, Society's mould, a heavy task. Strength is the mantra, a burden to bear, Vulnerability shunned, a silent despair.

Once, a canvas blank, dreams held so tight, Now, expectations loom, a suffocating night. Provider, protector, a never-ending chase, Emotions in check, a smile on his face.

The whispers of doubt, a relentless refrain, "Am I enough, can I ease the pain?" Sensitivity hidden, a weakness to quell, Yearning for connection, a truth yet to tell.

Lines blur in the grey, the path unclear, Gentle hearts yearned for, yet stoicism held dear. Fragile masculinity, a concept in flux, Redefining the role, is a desperate crux.

But a flicker remains, a fire within, To forge a new path, where kindness can win. Embrace vulnerability, a strength to unfold, A tapestry woven, new stories untold.

For in this era, of chaos and change, Men too can evolve, a beautiful range. Let compassion be armour, and empathy guide, In this complex dance, where humanity can confide.

13. Let me be selfish

"Selfishness is the joker card in a deck, it is meant to come to you in any sense"

The world, a steel fist, in a velvet glove, Whispers promises, fueled by self-love. A feast for the many, a morsel for some, Compassion a weakness, in this ruthless hum. Brotherhood crumbles, trust cracks and bleeds, and Survival's a ladder, sown with selfish deeds. Empathy's burden, a weight to cast off, Emotions a shield, deflecting life's scoff.
The climb is relentless, a scramble for air, Clawing and kicking, with hearts cold and bare. Morality's tether, a fraying rope thin, is Replaced by ambition, where victories win. Kindness, a whisper, lost in the roar, Sacrifice a fool's game, forevermore. Conscience is a traitor, a voice to subdue, For only the ruthless, can carve dreams anew.
But a shadow persists, a question that stings, Is this the true anthem, that humanity sings? Does love have no value, in this grand display? Is a life built on ashes, the only true way? Perhaps in the struggle, a choice can be made, To carve out a path, not entirely in shade. For cunning can partner, with kindness as a guide, A balance struck true, where both can reside.

Let ruthlessness sharpen, a tool for defence, But let love be the compass, for true consequence. This world may be harsh, a trial by fire, But within us resides, the power to inspire.

14. Money makes Money

"You always toss the coin of another man may it be faith, luck or hard work"

Worn shoes and hand-me-downs, a world in shades of grey,
He watched the rich kids laugh, their pockets filled with play.
Ice cream trucks a melody, just out of reach, it seemed, A
whispered yearning bloomed, a hunger to be redeemed.
A father's calloused hands, a mother's weary sigh, He saw the
weight of bills, a teardrop in their eye. "Money buys
freedom," a truth etched in his soul, A burning desire
ignited, to take back control.
He saw the shiny cars, the houses grand and tall, A world of
endless choices, a future to enthral. No more empty pockets,
no more longing stares, Just the power to purchase, and chase
away the cares.
The hunger grew within him, a fire fierce and bright, To
climb the ladder of success, with all his youthful might. He
dreamt of suits and briefcases, of deals and strategies, A
world where he could write his own, rewrite his family's
history.
The streets became his classroom, lessons learned each day,
The value of hard work, the hustle and the play. He saved his

pennies, pennies turned to dimes, The hunger for more, fueled by dreams on a dime.

But whispers of caution, a voice within him spoke, Of greed's cold grip, and the love that could be broken. For money is a tool, a means, not an end, And chasing riches blindly, could leave a broken friend.

So with a heart both hungry, and wise beyond his years, He vowed to chase his fortune, but leave no room for tears. For the things that truly matter, they cannot be bought, Love, family, and kindness, a wealth beyond all thought.

15. May the odds be in your favour

"Numerous days of failure can also be written as many days of lessons learnt"

The hand of fate, it dealt a strange twist, Fortune's smile, a crooked, curious kiss. Not riches untold, nor lands vast and grand, But favours peculiar, scattered like sand.
A crow on my shoulder, a constant dark guide, Whispers secrets in the wind, where others can't confide. Flowers bloom at my touch, in barren wastelands, A fleeting beauty, a mystery that expands.
Coins fall from pockets, unspent and unknown, A bottomless well, a fortune I've sown. Animals gather, a motley crew, Each with a talent, strange and new.
A talking raven, with wit sharp and keen, A loyal hyena, with laughter obscene. A one-eyed cat, with a gaze that can see, The secrets the world keeps, hidden from me.
Is this a blessing, or a twisted design? This life is off-kilter, where the ordinary can't shine. I yearn for normalcy, for life plain and clear, But fate's fickle hand holds me ever so near.
Perhaps there's a purpose, in this odd array, A hidden design, dawning each day. To bridge the unseen, a world in between,

Where magic and logic, on a tightrope convene.
So I'll face the odd, with a curious heart, Embrace the unknown, and play my strange part. For in this crooked smile, of fortune's cruel whim, There's a life less ordinary, waiting to begin.

16. De'throne

" Men taste success thrice in life, the first time he meets success he forgets to pay the EMI to stay on top every day"

The hand of fate, dealt a strange twist, Fortune's smile, a crooked, curious kiss. Not riches untold, nor lands vast and grand, But favours peculiar, scattered like sand.
A crow on my shoulder, a constant dark guide, Whispers secrets in the wind, where others can't confide. Flowers bloom at my touch, in barren wastelands, A fleeting beauty, a mystery that expands.
Coins fall from pockets, unspent and unknown, A bottomless well, a fortune I've sown. Animals gather, a motley crew, Each with a talent, strange and new.
A talking raven, with wit sharp and keen, A loyal hyena, with laughter obscene. A one-eyed cat, with a gaze that can see, The secrets the world keeps, hidden from me.
Is this a blessing, or a twisted design? This life is off-kilter, where the ordinary can't shine. I yearn for normalcy, for life plain and clear, But fate's fickle hand holds me ever so near.
Perhaps there's a purpose, in this odd array, A hidden design, dawning each day. To bridge the unseen, a world in between,

Where magic and logic, on a tightrope convene.
So I'll face the odd, with a curious heart, Embrace the failure,
and play my strange part.

17. The story of Henry

"Millions of stories burn as nightfalls, at dawn the ordinary man wakes up for his purpose he is born for"

Steel mill dawn, sky a bruise, Cigarette smoke hangs, a weary excuse. Coffee scalds the throat, a bitter embrace, Another day dawns, another rat race.
Muscles ache, a symphony of pain, Sweat a salty chorus, echoing the rain. Machines scream, a metallic ballet, Sparks dance a jig, on this concrete ballet.
Lunch break, a greasy spoon symphony, Burnt burgers and fries, a lukewarm apology. Coffee refills, black and grim, Fueling the furnace, limb by limb.
Work drags on, an endless loop, The clock a mocking jester, with a cruel whoop. Whistle blows at five, a release from the cage, But the weight remains, on this weary stage.
Barflies and loners, a chorus of despair, Whiskey burns down, a temporary prayer. Women with vacant eyes, and laughter that's thin, A fleeting escape, to numb the day's sin.
Stumble home, under a streetlight's harsh gaze, Another day conquered, in a minimum wage daze. Crash on the mattress, worn and threadbare, Dream of escape, to somewhere with

no care.

But dawn will return, with its relentless call, Back to the steel mill, to answer life's thrall. Just another cog, in the machine's cold grip, A man named Henry, with a soul on the slip.

18. Try once again

"Such days"

The ashtray overflows, a mountain of spent hope, Each cigarette butt, a dream choked by cheap smoke. Sun bleeds through the blinds and paints harsh lines on the floor, Another day dawns, another rejection at the door.
The script sits crumpled, a monument to failed art, Rejection slips stacked high, tearing a hole in my heart. My agent's voice, a sneer down the phone, a tired refrain, "Maybe try something else, buddy. This racket's a game."
The rent's due tomorrow, the fridge a barren wasteland, Pride used to be breakfast, but hunger's a demanding landlord. The mirror reflects a stranger, eyes hollow and dim, The fire in my belly, is reduced to a flickering whim.
The world's a parade of winners, flashing their shiny degrees, While I'm stuck on the sidewalk, hawking dreams nobody sees. The streets echo with laughter, a symphony of success, And here I stand, a discordant note, drowning in emptiness.
Maybe tonight's the night, the bottle, my only friend, To numb the ache of failure, pretend it'll all mend. But the truth is it sits heavy, a weight I can't outrun, Maybe success was a mirage, a battle I can't outrun.

But somewhere, a flicker, a spark in the dying light, A whisper that says, "Get up, you haven't lost the fight." One more rejection, one more day, what's the damn difference? Maybe tomorrow's the sunrise, maybe it's just indifference.

19. Meanwhile, A man is contented

"Start being humble, you might like it"

Busted out of the city, a one-way ticket in my fist, Left the
suit behind and traded it for a calloused, honest wrist. Dusty
diner coffee, bitter and black as my mood, New name
scribbled on a napkin, the old one misunderstood.
Fields stretched on forever, under a sun that didn't give a
damn, Learning to speak the language of dirt with a
calloused, sweating hand. My body ached, a symphony of
muscles long forgotten, Sweat and grime, a baptism, erasing
all the bullshit I bought.
Nights, stars smeared across a canvas of black, No deadlines
screaming, just the crickets chirping back. Fireflics pulsed
like cheap neon, a message I finally saw, The quiet whispered
secrets, a truth without a flaw.
Days bled into weeks, then months, the sun my only boss,
Hands cracked and strong, pulling life from the stubborn
boss. The earth's heartbeat thrummed under my boots, a
steady, coarse drum, Nature's melody, a lullaby that finally
numbed the bum.

Staring back from the well, a face creased with honest wear,
No longer chasing phantoms, a burden I no longer bear.
Lines etched by sweat and earth, a story etched in my skin,
The city slicker a ghost, a memory growing thin.
No dreams, just dirt beneath my nails and the wind in my
hair, Living in the now, a life stripped bare. In the silence of
the fields, under a sky so vast, I finally found myself, the
bullshit a thing of the past.

20. Meanwhile, A man is not

The clock hand crawls, a mocking, slow ballet, Each tick a hammer blow, another wasted day. The office walls, a beige and sterile tomb, My soul a dusty relic, lost in the daily gloom.
Papers pile high, a mountain of bureaucratic dread, Numbers dance on screens, a symphony of the unsaid. The fluorescent hum, a maddening, endless drone, Yearning for a tempest, a life yet to be known.
My tie, a noose of silk, constricting dreams unseen, The coffee, bitter dregs, fuel for the working machine. The boss, a bloated tick, sucking the lifeblood dry, While I, a cog forgotten, yearn for a tearful cry.
Lunch break arrives, a meagre sandwich and a park, Watching pigeons squabble, a mirror to my spark. The city's symphony, a cacophony of despair, Exhaust fumes and honking horns, a burden hard to bear.
Home, a lonely shoebox, walls closing in tight, Dinner, a frozen meal, swallowed under flickering light. The T.V. drones on, a mindless, flickering charade, A hollow echo of

laughter, a life I never had.

Sleep comes eventually, a restless, troubled friend, Dreams flicker and fade, a future without end. Will I wake tomorrow, to this same monotonous grind? Or will the spark ignite, a new purpose I can find?

21. Hello, Mr. Depression Again

Depression ain't some shrink's word, some fancy diagnosis. It's a goddamn anvil chained to your gut, a slow, steady drag down. Like waking up hungover every goddamn day, even if you haven't touched a drop.

The world turns outside, a technicolour movie, but you're stuck in black and white, a flickering silent film. Laughter sounds hollow, a distant echo down a tin tunnel. Food turns to ash in your mouth, every bite a chore.

The bed becomes your best friend, your worst enemy. A suffocating cocoon where the shadows whisper doubts. Getting up feels like climbing Mount Everest in molasses, every step a Herculean effort. There's a fog in your head, thoughts sluggish and grey. Creativity? Inspiration? Gone fishin', haven't seen 'em in weeks. Every task, every chore, feels like pushing a boulder uphill, only to watch it roll back down, crushing your spirit further.

The mirror shows a stranger, eyes dull and vacant. The spark in your soul dimmed to a flickering ember. Even anger, that glorious, hot-blooded bastard, feels like a distant memory. You're just... numb. A hollow shell going through the motions.

And the worst part? The goddamn guilt. The voice hisses, "Snap out of it, you lazy sack." But snapping out of it feels like trying to fly with broken wings. It ain't about weakness, it's about a war raging inside you, and you ain't sure whose side you're on.

22. Glass of whiskey & Pain

"Cheers as I was drunk when I wrote it"

The pain ain't some poet's metaphor, a bleeding rose or a wounded dove. It's a rusty knife twisting in your gut, a dull ache that settles in your bones like cheap wine. It ain't a clean break, a bone snapped sharp and sudden. It's a slow, simmering burn, a pot left on the stove too long, charring your insides. Sleep becomes a battlefield, dreams laced with barbed wire, waking up feeling like you wrestled a goddamn grizzly all night.

Laughter feels like sandpaper on a raw wound, sex a chore, a duty you owe your tired body. The world throbs around you, a technicolour nightmare, while you're stuck in the grimy back alley, black and white, the air thick with regret.

The booze, well, that's a different story. It doesn't dull it, not exactly. It just pours gasoline on the fire, making it burn brighter and hotter. But in that desperate, scorching heat, there's a strange kind of clarity. The whiskey becomes a hammer, pounding a rhythm against the ache, a counterpoint to the symphony of your misery.

It ain't a cure, mind you. No magic potion erases the scars. But with a good swig of amber fire, the pain becomes a companion, a twisted dance partner in the lonely hours. You clink glasses with it, a silent toast to the goddamn mess you've made of things.

The mirror shows a stranger, a roadmap of past battles etched on his face. His eyes were bloodshot, hair a mess, the ghost of a smile mocking him from past glories. It ain't about crying or screaming, some cathartic release. It's a silent scream trapped in your throat, a pressure building with nowhere to go.

But with the whiskey coursing through your veins, the scream finds a voice, a raspy growl that echoes in the empty room. It's a messy, ugly kind of honesty, but it's yours. The pain and the whiskey, a two-man brawl in a smoky bar, and for a fleeting moment, you feel a twisted kind of alive.

23. A glass of Love

"Cheers, I was sober when I wrote this"

Love ain't some sonnet whispered under a balcony, some fairy tale with a happily ever after. It's a goddamn battlefield, a messy tangle of sheets and sweat. It's a moth drawn to a flickering flame, knowing it'll get burned but diving in anyway.

You see her across the bar, a shot of tequila in a world of watered-down beer. There's a spark in her eyes, a wildness that mirrors the storm brewing in your soul. Maybe it's beauty, maybe it's trouble, hell, probably a bit of both. You can't look away, even if you know it's a recipe for disaster.

Conversations flow like cheap whiskey, raw and honest, laced with laughter and unspoken desires. You talk about the scars on your soul, the dreams that went up in smoke, and for some crazy reason, she doesn't flinch. Maybe she sees the flicker of something real beneath the cynicism, a kindred spirit drowning in the same sea of loneliness.

Suddenly, your crummy apartment doesn't seem so bad. The smell of stale beer and cigarettes takes on a strange comfort, a shared secret between you two. You wake up tangled in limbs, the morning light harsh and unforgiving, but there's a warmth beside you that chases away the chill.

But love, like a good bottle of bourbon, goes sour after a while. The fights get louder, fueled by jealousy and unspoken resentments. The passion turns to a simmering anger, a constant low hum beneath the surface. You look at her and see not just the beauty, but the flaws, the cracks in the facade.

And maybe, just maybe, you see the same flicker of doubt in her eyes. The realization that this crazy dance, this beautiful mess, might not have a happy ending. But even then, even in the wreckage, there's a grudging respect, a shared memory of the fire that once burned so bright.

Love ain't a promise, ain't forever. It's a fleeting moment of connection, a shared journey through the dark. It scars you, and leaves you raw and vulnerable, but for a while, it makes the goddamn emptiness bearable. And in the end, that might just be enough.

24. Jekyll or Hyde?

"Being a man is all about embracing and accepting your true nature"

They say you gotta be one thing, a clean line, a choice, Jekyll or Hyde predator or prey, find your goddamn voice. But me, I'm a mess, a tangled wire, a paradox walking free, Halfway hustle, halfway heartache, a bit of both, you see.

The Jekyll in me, teeth bared and claws unsheathed, Scrappin' for a living, on the streets my hunger bequeathed. A hustler's heart, a gambler's grin, chasing dreams in the night, Dodging shadows, playing dirty, under the flickering neon light.

But then the moon paints the alleys soft, and a different side appears, A yearning for comfort, a whisper brushing away the sneers. The hide unfurls a tender thing, wanting solace from the storm, Seeking shelter, a quiet corner to keep my body warm.

I crave connection, a gentle touch, a moment of tenderness shown, Poetry spilling from my lips, words I keep mostly unknown. The Jekyll growls, "This is weakness, a sucker's game to play," But the Hyde whispers back, "It's the only way to chase the blues away."

So I walk this tightrope, a Jekyll and Hyde in one, A contradiction roarin', a battle never truly won. But maybe that's

the beauty, the glorious, messy strife, To hold the darkness and the light, and dance between them in life.
The world wants labels, black and white, a hero or a villain's guise, But I'm a symphony of greys, a million flickering fireflies.
Jekyll and Hyde, two sides of the coin, scratchin' out a crooked rhyme, And in the dissonance I find my truth, existing one messy day at a time.

25. Mother's love at 25

She wasn't sunshine and roses, no Hallmark card schmaltz,
More like a dented teacup, chipped and stained but still
holding the warmth. Her love wasn't a spotlight, harsh and
blinding, but a flickering gaslight, Dim and unreliable, but
enough to see by in the grimy alleys of life.
We weren't a picture-perfect family, no staged smiles or
forced laughter, More like a pack of stray dogs, scrabbling for
scraps under a flickering streetlamp. She yelled, sure, a
banshee's wail that could curdle milk, But her anger was a
thunderstorm, fierce but brief, clearing the air for a grudging
truce.
Didn't say "I love you" much, choked on the damn words,
But it was there in the way she'd leave a plate of burnt toast
by your bed, In the way she never complained when you
pawned her good silver for a bottle, In the tired slump of her
shoulders when you landed in jail again.
No fairy tales, no unconditional bullshit. Her love was a
fistful of crumpled bills shoved in your pocket, A silent
prayer mumbled under her breath as you stumbled out the

door, A knowing look that said, "You damn fool, you'll be back," and you always were.

Maybe she wasn't perfect, hell, nobody is, But her love, it was real, a gritty, grimy diamond in the rough. Flawed, yes, like a chipped teacup, but it held the warmth, And in this cold, unforgiving world, that warmth, that was all that mattered, all that was enough.

26. Dad's letter

" The Old man knows to write when its the right time. period"

Son,

Don't expect sugar-coated bullshit in this letter. Life ain't a goddamn fairytale, and neither am I. This ain't no apology, either. I raised you the way I knew best, knuckles rapping on your head when you screwed up, a boot to your backside when you needed it most.

Maybe it wasn't hugs and bedtime stories. Maybe it was the smell of motor oil on my hands and the constant cussing under my breath. We weren't father-son pals sipping beers on the porch swing. We were two goddamn gears in the same rusty machine, grinding away at survival.

You left, a storm cloud bursting out the front door, slamming it like a gunshot. Took your anger with you, a jagged piece of me you ripped away. You called it a loveless house, a cage. Maybe it was, but it was the only goddamn cage I knew how to build.

Now what? You're out there in the jungle, teeth bared, ready to take on the world. But the world, son, it's a scrapyard, full of broken dreams and rusted promises. They'll see that fire in your eyes, that chip on your shoulder, and they'll try to use it. Don't be a goddamn fool.

Listen, life ain't about proving anything to anyone, least of all me. It's about carving out your own damn path, laying down your own bricks, even if they ain't perfect. Screw the fancy degrees and the shiny suits. Find something that makes your blood sing, something that gets you out of bed in the morning even when your bones ache.

Don't come crawling back with your tail between your legs, expecting a warm welcome and a pat on the head. I won't be here. But if you do figure it out, if you build something real, something that matters, then that's enough. That's the closest you'll ever get to an "I'm proud of you" from me.

So go on, get out there and fight. Fight for what you believe in, even if it's just the right to exist on your own damn terms. Just promise me you won't go down without a goddamn fight. Your old man,

(Signed with a shaky hand and a single faded teardrop smudging the ink)

27. The great degree

The diploma, a flimsy sheet, a gilded cage, a paper crown,
Hanging on the wall, mocking with its empty, sterile sound.
Four years of lectures, a mountain of forgotten facts, Did
they teach you how to live, navigate the city's cracks?
Professors droned on, voices muffled by a beer haze,
Spouting theories on life, living from a book-lined maze. But
life, my friend, ain't a sonnet, neatly structured and polite,
It's a barroom brawl, a drunken stumble through the
flickering night.
The real teachers wear scars, not tweed jackets and ties, The
bartender with a weary smile, the hustler with knowing eyes.
The waitress juggling plates, dreams fading with each passing
year, They'll teach you grit, resilience, the sting of a silent
tear.
The city itself, a concrete jungle, a symphony of honks and
screams, Will show you the beauty in broken things, the
poetry in shattered dreams. The drunk passed out on a park
bench, the lovers whispering in the rain, They'll teach you
empathy, the weight of joy, the sting of pain.
So toss that diploma in the trash, a meaningless piece of
paper thin, The real lessons are learned on the streets, where
life throws you in. You'll graduate with callouses, not a fancy
Latin phrase, A degree in the school of hard knocks, living

life in a whiskey daze.
Because the world doesn't care about your GPA or your fancy
degree, It wants to see the fire in your eyes, the fight you hold
within thee. So go out there, get bruised, get lost, get back
up with a defiant grin, Life's the only real teacher, my friend,
and its lessons never end.

28. Women who become poetries

She wasn't a porcelain doll, all sugar and spice, More like a shot of tequila, burning slow and twice. Eyes like a smoky barroom, secrets swirling in the haze, A smile that could disarm you, then leave you in a daze.
Her body, a roadmap of stories, each scar a battle won, Not a perfect sculpture, but a symphony on the run. Hands that could caress you one moment, then slap you the next, A fierce independence burning in her restless, fire-kissed chest. She wasn't a damsel in distress, waiting for some knight to appear, More like a hurricane in stilettos, with a heart both fierce and clear. She'd laugh at your pathetic poems, then write her own in the dead of night, A challenge and a muse, a beautiful, maddening sight.
Love with her wasn't a fairytale, a happily ever after dream, More like a tango in a smoky room, fueled by lust's flickering gleam. Passionate fights that left the sheets tangled and the air thick with desire, A love that burned bright and quick, a flame that could set your soul on fire.
She wouldn't be your savior, wouldn't fix your broken wings, But she might fly alongside you, for a while, on damaged, beautiful things. And when it all ended, in a messy, tear-stained goodbye, She'd leave you with a memory, a

bittersweet lullaby.

29. Women who become stories

She ain't no doe-eyed dreamer, no princess in a tower of sighs, This woman, she's seen the world, the bloodshot truth in weary eyes. Love for her ain't some sonnet, a whispered promise in the dark, It's a calloused hand in yours, a shared burden in the park.

Her scars tell stories, etched by battles fought and won, Not battles for some prince, but for survival, under a blood-red sun. She's tasted loneliness, a bitter pill on a hungry tongue, But learned to find solace in herself, a strength where she once felt young.

Love for her ain't fireworks, a fleeting spark that burns so bright, It's the quiet ember glowing, a warmth that chases away the night. It's seeing you raw and flawed, the darkness hidden deep within, And choosing to stay beside you, a love that lets the healing begin.

She won't sugarcoat your demons, won't pat you on the head and coo, She'll call you out on your bullshit, a truth you might not want to construe. But in that brutal honesty, a love that's fierce and true, A love that says, "I see you, all of you, and I choose you."

Love for her ain't a cage, a gilded prison built for two, It's a shared journey, a dance with shadows, seeing you through and through. It's respecting your freedom, even when it means you might stray, Trusting you'll return, knowing the love will always stay.

She ain't perfect, hell, nobody is, but her love, it's a fortress strong, A weathered shield against the world, where you truly belong. So don't expect grand pronouncements, no tearful declarations grand, Just the quiet comfort in her presence, a love that understands.

30. Take care

in the caverns of your bones, a universe hums.
galaxies of possibility, whispering constellations of worth.
don't let the world dim your light. you are your own sun.
let your scars be silver linings, stitches that hold you whole.
love the curve of your hips, the song your laughter sings.
you are a masterpiece, still under construction, but beautiful
nonetheless.
forgive yourself, the way you forgive the changing seasons.
grow, bloom, wilt, become again.
you are enough, exactly as you are.

31. Broken craft

"All he wanted was a home"

they see him,
a mountain, broad shoulders,
a fortress built

against the world's storms.
they don't see
the calloused hands
cradle a wilting flower,
whisper life back
into its fragile stem.
they don't see
the tears welling up
at a sad movie,
masked by a cough
and a gruff "stupid dust.
the world sees him
as a force, unyielding,
but we see the man,
a heart wrapped in granite.

32. Expectations

grey creeping in at the temples,

a mirror reflecting
a stranger with a familiar face.
the suit, once a badge,
now feels like a cage,
the climb to the top
a summit leaving him breathless,
but what's the view?
questions like weeds
through the cracks of certainty,
"Who am I?"
a whisper echoing in the hollow halls
of his success.
a map with faded ink,
the destination unclear,
a yearning for a compass
pointing not to wealth,
but to a life that feels real.
the world sees him
as a titan, unbending,
but his soul craves
a wild, uncharted journey,
to rediscover the man
beneath the expectations.

33. A silent plea

mirror the lines etched on their faces,

years of work,

a silent conversation

of sacrifice.

his dreams,

feathers adrift in a restless wind,

haven't yet landed

on the golden nest

they built with sweat and prayer.

each sunrise,

a battle with guilt,

the weight of their hopeful eyes

a constant echo

in the hollow halls of his doubt.

he whispers promises

to a moonlit sky,

"one day, I'll make you proud,"

a silent plea

to bridge the gap between dreams and reality.

love,

a double-edged sword,

cuts him deep,

wanting nothing more

than to be the sun in their twilight years.

34. Heal

Stale coffee sweats in a chipped mug,
mirror shows a face time punched too much.
Scars ain't just on knuckles, some run deeper,
childhood ghosts that whisper, shadows that creep up.
We build these walls, brick by bottled rage,
a fortress of silence on a lonely stage.
Drink to numb the ache, pretend we're alright,
but the cracks in the plaster show the fight we fight.
Every man's a battlefield, some wars you win,
some leave you hollow, a shell caved in.
But healing ain't weakness, ain't some touchy-feely crap,
it's facing the demons, taking a long, hard rap.
Talk it out, scream it loud, let the tears finally fall,
ain't no shame in breaking, that's how we stand tall.
Sunlight can't reach the garden if the weeds take hold,
gotta rip them out, and let the new flowers unfold.
So ditch the whiskey, the bravado, the act,
let your guard down, mend the cracks in the pact.
Healing ain't pretty and might leave you raw and sore,
but the man who faces his demons can finally explore.

This ain't some touchy-feely bullshit hearts and flowers,
it's about facing the storm, weathering the dark hours.
Because a healed man, a man who lets go,
that's the strongest soldier the world will ever know.

35. Comeback

"The world shall always throw a stone and bruise
your ego"

muscles ache,
a map of battles fought,
some won, some scars
etched deep in his skin.
the world throws stones,

bruises his ego,
whispers doubt
like a cold wind.
but within him,
a fire still embers,
a defiance, a strength
older than time.
he's fallen,
kissed the dust,
but the sunrise
finds him rising again.
tears may fall,
a cleansing rain,

but they water the seeds
of a will that won't wane.
for every man
holds the power to mend,
to rise from the ashes,
a phoenix, a friend
to his own broken heart.
not perfect, but whole,
scars a testament
to the strength of his soul.

36. Emotions are like rivers

I feel everything, and dont feel sorry about it, its a river and shall flow within its vein

Anger

a shadow simmers,
beneath the surface, calm,
a clenched fist, a white-knuckled grip
on a world that feels off-kilter.

words, once whispers of comfort,

now barbed arrows,
shot from a heart-turned-fortress,
defending a wound unseen.

anger, a coiled serpent,
hisses in his chest,
poison seeping
into the air, he breathes.

a storm brews in his eyes,
a silent tempest,
yearning for release,
a cleansing rain for his parched soul.

but somewhere beneath the rage,
a flicker of hurt,
a yearning for solace,

a broken compass seeking true north.

for even a man
forged in fire,
holds a heart
that aches to be understood.

Happiness

sunrise paints his face gold,
a tired smile, a genuine fold
at the corner of his eyes.

his calloused hands,

once instruments of work,
now cradle a steaming cup,
a simple pleasure,
a quiet sup.

laughter, a melody
rarely heard,
breaks free from his lips,
a bird taking flight.

the weight on his shoulders,
a constant companion,
feels lighter today,
a feather in the summer breeze.

contentment, a warm sunbeam,
melts the ice around his heart,

a quiet joy,
a masterpiece painted with small parts.

for a man's happiness,
unlike a mountain grand,
can be found in the pebbles,
held close in his hand.

Sadness

salt stains his pillow,
oceans welling in eyes,
a storm brewing
behind a stoic guise.

a heavy sigh,

the exhale of a burdened soul,
a weight on his chest,
a story yet untold.

words trapped like birds
in a cage of pride,
longing to take flight,
but fear keeps them tied.

the world sees him
as a fortress, unyielding,
but behind the walls,
a fragile heart, reeling.

sadness, a slow burn,
embers glowing in the dark,
a teardrop escapes,

a silent, falling spark.

for even the strongest oak,
with roots that run deep,
can bend in the wind,
and softly weep.

Surprise

surprise, a hummingbird's wings,
fluttering in his chest,
a jolt, a current
disrupting his usual rest.

eyes widen,

a child's curiosity reborn,
the world, once a canvas
in shades of beige and worn,

suddenly splashed
with vibrant hues unseen,
a melody unheard,
a note, crisp and clean.

a smile, hesitant at first,
then blooming, wide and true,
a crack in his armor,
revealing a brand new hue.

surprise, a whisper
that life can still surprise,
a chance encounter,

a twinkle in new eyes.

for even the most jaded soul,
etched with lines of time,
can find a spark of wonder,
in the unexpected rhyme

Fear

knuckles white,
gripping the air,
a silent scream
no words can dare

to utter. fear,
a serpent cold,
coiling tight
around his soul.

a shadow creeps,
whispers doubt in his ear,
painting futures
dark and unclear.

his bravado, a mask,
cracks and starts to peel,
a vulnerability
he struggles to conceal.

the world sees him
as a mountain, strong and tall,
but fear can bring
even giants to fall.

a silent plea

to a sky vast,

for the courage to rise,

let the trembling subside.

for even the bravest heart,

though clad in steel and might,

trembles in the darkness,

fearing the coming night.

37. Chivalry is not yet death

Forget knights in shining armour, all that prancing and such, Chivalry ain't about dying young, it's about giving a damn, that much.

It ain't about damsels in distress, though helping a lady ain't a crime, More like opening a door, offering a ride, respecting her space and time.

Chivalry's a bowling courtesy, like letting the other guy go first, Even if you're hot to knock down those pins and quench your competitive thirst.

It's about holding your ground, man, standing up for what's right, Like telling that jerk Lebowski to take his aggression and shove it outta sight.

Chivalry ain't about fighting duels or wearing a goddamn codpiece, It's about treating everyone decent, even if they're a total freaking weasel.

It's about a handshake that means something, a promise you aim to keep, Like returning a borrowed rug, even if it's the wrong damn colour, man, that's deep.

Chivalry's about loyalty, to your friends, your word, your bowling team, Like standing by Walter, even if he's freaking out about a rug, it's a crazy dream.

So next time you see someone struggling, lend a hand, offer a drink, Chivalry ain't dead, man, it's just the way decent folks on the planet think.

38. Bravery

not muscles,
but the tremor in his voice
calling home,
a whisper across continents.
not scars,
but the way his hand
holds hers a little tighter,
knowing every goodbye
could be forever.
not medals,
but the ache in his bones
carrying the weight
of a world not his own.
brave
isn't the absence of fear,
but the courage to
love in the face of it.

39. Men.

To the Men Who Carry the World,
There's a quiet strength in your sunrise routine,
the coffee brewing, the silent goodbyes
kissed on foreheads, mumbled promises
to return before the fireflies ignite the skies.
We see the callouses etched on your hands,
stories whispered in the language of hard work,
building, fixing, holding on tight to dreams,
even when the world throws its heaviest burdens.
You are the lighthouse in the storm,
a steady beam guiding us home,
shouldering burdens unseen,
fighting battles fought all alone.
You faced the demons in the dead of night,
wrestled with doubts bathed in the pale moonlight,
but rose with the sun, a warrior disguised,
wearing a smile, shielding us from your fight.
The world may not sing your praises loudly,
but know this, dear men, you stand so proud.
In the quiet moments, when the day is done,
we see the love, the battles you've won.
You are the partners, the fathers, the rock,
the husbands who weather every shock.

Your strength, a silent symphony,

a love that sets our spirits free.

So keep fighting, keep striving, and keep holding on,

your resilience is a beautiful dawn.

We see you, we honor you, every single day,

for in your journey, you light our way.

With love and admiration,

The ones who see your worth.

40.

• 84 •

Life should come from you and not at you.

Timothée Hal Chalamet ”

www.ingramcontent.com/pod-product-compliance
Lightning Source LLC
Chambersburg PA
CBHW021114130726
47988CB00003B/1019